C000152950

73

This Is How We Disappear

છ૪

poems by Titilope Sonuga

Write Bloody North

writebloodynorth.ca

Copyright © Titilope Sonuga, 2019.

All rights reserved. No part of this book may be used, performed, or reproduced in any manner whatsoever without written permission from the publisher except in the case of brief quotations embodied in critical articles or reviews.

First edition.
ISBN: 978-0992024536

Cover Design by Katrina Noble
Interior Layout by Winona León
Edited by Alessandra Naccarato
Proofread by Keaton Maddox
Author Photo by Kosol Onwudinjor

Type set in Bergamo from www.theleagueofmoveabletype.com

Write Bloody North
Toronto, ON

Support Independent Presses
writebloodynorth.ca

THIS IS HOW WE DISAPPEAR

THIS IS HOW WE DISAPPEAR

Missing

We Are Ready

Lessons in Summer

Things We Learned By Blood

Homegoing

MISSING

*[They] were ordinary girls, young enough to be my daughters,
who had been raised to almost mythic status
by their extraordinary experience.*

—Helon Habila, *The Chibok Girls*

THEY ARE STILL LAUGHING

In the dream,
I close my eyes and count backward from 276.
The girls crawl feet first from their hiding places,
some from behind the curtains where their hands
stuck out, others from under the bed,
untangling a mess of limbs.

A slit in the silence bursts
and their voices fall out.
They call each other's names,
unlearning memory,
bones melting back to whole.

The ones who do not make it into hiding,
shake their bodies loose
from where they stood suspended in time.

They brush past me as they go,
peeling back the skin of a thousand blackened days,
calling up the blood to dance
beneath their former faces, the ones still soft enough
for their mothers to recognize.

This time when a girl walks into a forest,
real or imagined,
when her body kisses the earth
like a felled tree,
everybody hears it.

We go deaf with the hearing,
even if she never makes a sound.

THE HISTORY BOOKS WILL REMEMBER

Girls the size of a small tribe vanished
like a twisted kind of hide and seek.

We began our counting too late.
Imagined them giggling in their hiding places

like the games we played
when we were just small girls,
sure someone would find us

no matter how far we went,
no matter how dark the night.

Missing

As much as I wish to, the president said,
    I cannot promise that we can find them.

They converted to Islam,
married off to the fighters, Abubakar Shekau said.

They were taken
across the border into Cameroon, witnesses said.

A negotiator told us, *At least three died*
in the early days, from a snake bite,
malaria and dysentery.

I'm outraged and heartbroken, Michelle Obama
posted a picture of herself holding a sign.

Please know this, Malala Yousafzai wrote,
we will never forget you.

Years passed without a whisper from the girls.

★

My father's gun
in the upstairs closet will shoot
its first and only shot
when I am ten and the armed robbers come
rattling our gate like rabid dogs.
My three sisters and I huddled in our nightgowns
on his bedroom floor.

We have to leave this country, he whispers
to my mother, his finger trembling
on the trigger.

That night my father will almost kill a man
to protect our childhood.
He will never say the words *I love you*
but in the chamber of his heart
is one loaded bullet.

★

Midnight at the water's edge.

Blessing and 3,000 refugees wade in,
silent and barefoot.

They fall into the sea.
Soon, most will wash back ashore
with no name to call
but the numbers scribbled on their clothes.

For weeks, the smuggler's telephones
on the other side, silent.

No one to answer for the girls,
with skin like rich palm oil
bloodying the water.

★

They built fences in Morocco,
paid the nations on the coastline
to keep the teeming bodies back.

> *Tomorrow, Europe might no longer*
> *be European*, said Qaddafi.

We will use human beings as weapons,
cram the black bodies into fishing trawlers,
launch them from Libya into the sea.
The ungovernable,
the slaves,
the concubines and prostitutes,

burn it to the ground.

*

Swift flowing river
snakes its way through the heart of Edmonton
to lay still
in the winter of our arrival.

Our hands turn white,
the air like shards of glass to our faces.

That night, our family shares
a pizza in our basement apartment.
Then we fall asleep, three on the bed,
three on the floor,
our bellies bloated with hope.

We tread water for twenty winters
between our yesterdays
and the tomorrow we were promised.

*

Everything here is borrowed
or stolen:
the language, the land.

My own body,
far flung.

I lose my old English,
my tongue twice colonized.

*

All the women I know are running
toward, or away,
and everything I know of disappearance
begins with water.

The girls,
their thirsty mouths open skyward,
rainwater muddying the forest floor.

The six-month ocean crossing
that pulls the salt from our skin.

The dam
breaking inside my mother.

The first blood sacrifice
that pulled me from one world into the next
began inside a woman,
sliced down the middle,
so another woman could emerge whole.

All I know of magic making and survival
I learnt at birth.

*

I want to defend my country.

Which one?

I mythologize my grandmother, write stories
about warrior women
with thunder between their thighs.

Then the girls disappear, and no one goes looking.
I ask my mother
the Yoruba word for shame.

>   *Do you know they only drank water when it rained?*

>   *What kind of country does nothing
>   when two hundred girls
>   disappear?*

A thousand Indigenous women
stop in their tracks
to crane their necks back in unison.

Tears flood the highway
till even the rivers overflow.

*

The girls had disappeared for three weeks
before we knew their names.

Then we spoke them: two hundred
and seventy-six in Chibok,

but thousands more, missing and murdered
across the country, answered.

*

It is customary to wait seven days
to name a child.

Touch her lips
with water and palm oil,
honey and salt,
kola,
give her a taste of the bitter
and the sweet,
the joy and the pain.

Pray for her a spirit
with the resilience of water.

All of this just to say:
Stay.

WE DREW CHIBOK ON THE MAP IN OUR BLOOD

dis·ap·pear /disə'pir / verb: /

I.

the men, thick as baobab, become a forest, drag us in by the wild of our hair

II.

the men scratch our names from our throats
betray our bodies
bones bend back
break

III.

we become a whisper
hands gather a scream
back into her mouth
pray
the only way we know how
palms clasped and reaching
elbow deep into a soft night

IV.

beg god between her legs
birth and bury
what we must to stay alive

silent stream
silk fish swirl
a red amen around our ankles

V.

beneath the moon that sees us all
our mother prays into the black
bloom between her legs
reaches deep to birth us back
red scream
names we no longer answer to

VI.

we scatter from her hands
silk fish swirl
in a wild stream.

IN THE HOWLING HOUSE

My sister is a furious mourning,
a mark on everything living.
We search the huts,
lift the men's limbs one by one,
but there is no blood to mark the taking.

One hand points to Sambisa,
his finger draws a crooked line that cracks
the village in two.

From beneath the parched earth
a handful of girls return,
a school of slippery fish,
their memory scales on their tongues
iridescent, changing with each passing light.

They cannot remember now
if she jumped too, or if it was her voice
they heard pinned down by a blade's edge.

Our father who is not in heaven
was hallowed then hollowed
from years of waiting at the door for a knock
that never came; we seek and do not find,
we ask and no one answers.

Our mother no longer calls God by name,
attends neither prayer nor protest
to wail on cue. Her grief is a snake coiled
in her belly, in the space where her daughter
once was. She spits the poison
at the nightmare that awakens another.
Time lunges forward and my sister is still gone,
yet I am here with a face just like her own.

All our blood races toward the open wound,
rushes to retrieve what has been severed,
the phantom limb always more persistent
than the living.

I become a murmur in a howling house,
where every night we chant our grief
into our prayer mats, while the furious ghosts
of a million missing girls
lament at the school room door.

Visiting Day
Federal Government College–Bun Yadi, February 25, 2014

In the teachers' lounge
the television is a quiet hum.
The president is on again,
his smile wide as a wail.

The news is always the same:
all is well
and oil is still well and pumping furiously
through our country's veins.

Tonight, the boarding school is quiet.
Everything is as the children left it.
The row of polished shoes at the door,
the food provisions uneaten,
uniforms ironed and ready.

No one startles the splay of young bodies
in deep sleep, or breaks into the school
with fury on their tongues,
machete claws sharpened,
their teeth a row of bullets.

In the morning,
the bell rings and everyone is alive.
Their voices fill the halls
as they clang their metal buckets
rushing to their baths.

No one's mother is ragged with grief,
and nobody's father is dragging politicians
from their beds into the streets,
wielding questions like batons,
demanding more than wringing hands
and more prayer.

Nobody even knows the name
of a boarding school in Bun Yadi
where the children slept safe in their beds last night,
dreaming a kaleidoscope of color,
the night sky full of promise.

No one is draped in black,
mourning a morning that never came.

We laugh loud
from throats that haven't been slit open,
kiss our babies on both cheeks
and marvel at our good fortune.

HIDE AND SEEK
Bama Hospital Camp, 2015

It begins with a sleight of hand,
fingers that move so quickly
it's almost like it didn't happen:

> *"They give you food, but in the night they come back."*

From the hand
rice appears like a shimmering coin.

Inside the coin, the currency of survival,
a secret
inside the secret, a spinning bottle,
a flattened village nestled inside.

Inside the village
men in uniform who come to rescue
their mouths a cage.

Inside the cage
girl
after girl
the size of a small mistake.

Inside the girl
a light going out.

No Place Left to Bury the Dead

What do we do with the bodies?
How do we gather them up
to know which arm goes where?
Whose eyes are still searching?
Whose head with the delicate head tie
now sits atop a suited torso?
Which hands clasped in prayer belongs
to which kneeling body?
Whose heart is this,
and to whose hollowed chest does it belong?
How do we return the boys to their fathers?
Who will reconstruct the jigsaw
of teeth and flesh?
What do we give back to the mothers?
Who will fish out the ears from this blood?
Who will travel this bleeding river
to find her children
whole enough to call by name?

WE MAKE HEAVEN AT SUNDAY MARKET

In Konduga,
they sent two women to market
with a promise of eternity
strapped to their chests.

It was already too late to scream
if anyone had noticed them,
there was no difference between
the desperate gestures of a bargain unfolding
and the two arms floating up,
synchronized swimmers in a pool
of desperate bodies.

Before the peculiar thunder and blood rain,
everything was as it should have been.

One woman bought an apple first,
sunk her teeth into it,
something sweet before
the promise of heaven
on a Sunday morning.

The other woman stopped
to run a finger over the gutted fish,
flicking their scales,
silver coins into a wishing well.

THE GIRL COMES BACK WITH FIRE IN HER CHEST

I.

By what name do we call the girl
when she comes back?

Is it cruel now to call her Joy,
        to call her Precious,
        to call her Patience?

Do we turn her old clothes to rags
to wash her with, or break
the bed where her feet now dangle
and burn it to ash?

Do we sing a praise song or dirge
when the girl comes back,
with her mouth sewn shut
and her eyes sunken in?

Do we welcome her home
where there is none
and forget how savage the privilege of weeping
before the one whose tears have dried up?

When the girl comes back,
whose arms does she run into?
Who will call her daughter
and call her daughter *daughter* too?
Whose milk has not yet curdled?
Who will soothe this broken woman
back to girl:

        Precious, Patience

and back to whole again?

II.

The girl's mouth pools with blood from her razor tongue
in the market with her hands held high she becomes a wall
savors the anger like fruit she stole when no one was looking
tells her sins to God, no one is listening

in the market with her hands held high she becomes a wall
becomes a fire no one can touch
tells her sins to God, no one is listening
she is alone here

becomes a fire no one can touch
savors the anger like fruit she stole when no one was looking
she is alone here
The woman's mouth pools with blood from her razor tongue

III.

At the mosque in Mubi,

no one could say which one of them
held the baby or the bomb,

each cradled a heavy head
held its body across her chest
beneath a billowing cloth.

Both walked with the grace only mothering teaches,
moving without disturbing a sleeping thing.

When we were putting the pieces back together,
trying to bury what we could not name,
there was no one left,
not even a child
to tell us which mother they heard ticking
or clucking before they knelt.

We could not bend the bones back from broken
to know whose forehead touched the ground last
or gather the breath back into their mouths,
even into a mumble, to say
whose prayer was answered first,

whose daughter went home.

AFTER SHE IS GONE

Death does not glance back
at the cries of the living.

We do not know what finally calls the sprit
out of the body,
or whose cruel hands draw the promise
of a lifetime into a lifeline.

No poem or prayer prepares you for this:
a lifetime of standing in the gap,
somewhere between here and the hereafter,
neither living nor dead,
a ghost even to yourself.

WE ARE READY

WE ARE READY

Commissioned Poem, Presented at the inauguration of President Muhammadu
Buhari, (Baba) May 29, 2015, Eagle Square, Abuja.

They said they heard a war
growling in our bellies
said we had a taste for blood
imagined us clawing apart the country
hungry and greedy

they said the Giant of Africa
had nursed her growing pains too long
bones creaking and stretching to hold still
the tremble of fault lines
across land mass
across language
across tribe
across religion

they said our voices were too small to be heard
over the noise of bombs
over the noise of pundits
with predictions about chaos and carnage
oil gushing from our open wounds
they said we were not ready

but maybe
it was something in the wind
maybe we caught the scent of an old promise
and remembered something familiar as freedom
an unrelenting irrational hope
demanding answers for generations waiting
bodies hunched like question marks
beneath an angry sun

on that day
we dared even lightning to touch us
dared the rain to wash away our resolve
as we bloomed defiant

across the country
purple thumbs sprung up
to affirm something greater than our differences
something too urgent to wait

from the cobwebs of every forgotten place
we came
said we are here

count us
remember our names

bruised and broken though we may be
we know how to heal
and heal again
how to reinvent in times of nothing
dance beneath the weight
of what threatens to break
our backs, how to pull laughter from our throats
when wailing was expected

children of Niger River current, running
of salt water swamp, and swelling plateau
of rock might and iron will
we have not forgotten
what was birthed between the push
of waterfall and savannah

what dreams were spoken
with 500 tongues
from hilltop and ocean belly
what tireless hands built this place
from soil and sweat

Baba, now that you are there
perched on the promise of tomorrow
propelled forward
by the hope of generations

remember the forgotten
the left behind
the left in the dark
the ones who carry the hope
of this country like a prayer
each individual pulse
of the heartbeat of this land
aching for someone to believe in

remember every square kilometer
pulsing with the bloodlines of millions
and millions more before us
bracing up the earth beneath our feet
so that we can walk in this moment
when the whole world will remember
how the multitudes became one
to say:

yes
this country belongs to us
complex and flawed
pushed to the brink then back again
but we are not ashamed
we are not afraid of the difficult journey
if change is here then we are ready

AFTER

2017: President Muhammadu Buhari remains silent during one hundred days of foreign medical leave in London.

Years from now, Baba,
the sky will still remember how the smoke rose,
the whole country a boiling pot.

In your absence
we count the passing days
by the abacus of the baby's ribs,
measure our rations by fists
on the kitchen floor
even the rats would have left.

The sun will still imitate fire
and we will turn our leathered faces
to the sky
searching for answers that do not come.
We will not ask what we already know:
no one is coming to save us.

Everything bakes back to the dust
it came from,
bodies suspend in time across the country.
Some in the towns
where the girls disappeared,
some at the bank
where the printers stopped running.
The rest,
a stack of bones still standing in line
at the petrol station,
their desperate fingers clutching
the empty jerry cans.

*

In Borno
the women are back in the kitchen doubled over.
They are back in their bedrooms in Bauchi
where the babies were snatched
from their arms and from their bellies.
The ache folds time into itself.

In Yobe the men still know
how it felt to make fists,
to knock on doors
the day before the taking.
They still shook hands
with their neighbors in the streets,
the missing limbs refuse to be forgotten.

Forgiveness is a thing we buried in the ground,
old bones we count just to be sure
that it happened, it was real.

*

Baba, now that you are there, perched on the promise
of tomorrow, propelled by the hope of generations,
do you still hear the song in the streets?
Do you lean down from your throne to press your ear
to the ground and catch its rhythm? Its timbre,
so much like regret. We sing a new song now
to fill the silence where your voice should have been,
to carry us through days that feel like endless night.
We do not sleep. We are afraid of losing even our dreams.
When there is nothing left, we paint pictures with our own blood,
snatch the beat from our chests to make music,
to make art, to make love, to drown out the noise
of bones crunching in the mouth,
of bulldozers come to eat what we starve to create.
And the children are falling, wilted flowers in the heat.
They are growing into men who have only known hunger,
who have been whittling their ribs into spears,
sharpening their teeth with their rage.
They are ready Baba, now that you are there,
to bite back the hand that has never fed them.

Lessons in Summer

LESSONS IN SUMMER

I.

In the summer of my new body,
a boy
whose hands make my blood bloom
beneath the skin.

He is gentle, so I am not afraid
when he plucks me up
like ripe and ready fruit.

It is the season of discovery
and we have spent many days like this.
Lying in the field of our wanting,
mapping the landscape of skin
with open palms; some borders

we promise not to cross.

II.

In class,
my physics professor speaks
past my empty seat.
She is teaching a lesson about gravity
that I already know
from the well of this boy's eyes.

I should be there learning about force,
the power of inertia.

I should be listening to the tricky dynamics
of two bodies, when one

is bigger and faster than me.

III.

It is summer and I am naked
with the boy I love,
pressing both hands against the wall
of his chest,
pleading with my eyes.

I forget to say no with my mouth.
I'm busy
trying to squeeze the useless gate of my legs
closed like my mother told me to.

Defiant tears roll down the cliff
of my face, the little girl inside me
falls to her death.

He is giggling in my ear
like he already knows the punch line
to a joke I will never tell.

IV.

Years later,

bent over the tub washing my hair,
my fingernails scrape my scalp
and drag the memory out of my head.

The dam breaches
and pain surges forward
through the scar, water everywhere
till I am drenched in it
on the bathroom floor,
hair clumped and mad.

I speak his name
and the wound breathes shut.

WE BLEED AND BLEED AND DO NOT DIE

When her eight-year-old comes
clutching the red siren wail of her dress,
she sweeps the tears from her face
and drags a finger slow across her lips.

They throw away the key,
tell no one.

Set the dress on fire with the rubbish pile,
watch the secret dance in the flames,
hear it cackle.

When she turns thirteen
there are no more dresses to burn.

Her father kills a chicken to celebrate.
They watch the knife slide quiet
across its neck like a secret
only blood knows.

The sharks come draped in white,
circle the table with their caps
in their hands.

They snap the wings first,
and she does not flinch,
does not hear the bones crack
between their teeth

when they drag the flesh
into their laughing mouths.

PEA

Memory curls at the edges,
yellows in the brain.
A picture forgotten
between the ridges of an old album.

The right hands know
how to peel
gently, sweep clean
the dust of buried things.

He parts your legs,
does not flinch,
runs a finger across
the pursed lips of the scar,
presses his to it:
a prayer.

Your mouth flies open,
a hallelujah,
sends the pictures tumbling out:

little girl
yellow dress
crooked red door
a room
wringing hands
dishrag your mouth

Pain suspends you in time then,
against the metal edge
of blood and blade,
a slice.

You are a woman now
on the other side of the globe,
safe beneath the soft touch of a lover
with gentle eyes that does not ask
childish questions with no answers,
like what would anyone
possibly want
with something the size
of a pea?

MILK

Bọlá's milk never stops coming
and for days after we cannot move her
from the bathroom floor.
We watch the tears tumble down her face,
she folds and unfolds the ọ̀já in her lap,

shirt hardened with crust,
milk stains on both breasts
like two small heads resting on her chest.

They bury the babies quick,
she cannot attend
Èèwọ̀ ni kí abiyamọ mọ sàárè ọmọ rẹ̀
a mother does not put her child's body in the ground
Èèwọ̀ ni
it is not done

We give away the unused diapers,
take the bags of clothes
lined up like tiny tombstones.

Bọlá is a walking graveyard,
a mouth that lays to rest the oríkì
whispered into the soft folds of skin,
arms that still feel the weight
of two ten-pound bodies.

We tell her, *Time heals all.*
She listens.
We tell her, *God knows best.*
She nods.

Her tears eventually slow, then stop.
It looks like acceptance.
She does not tell us
that she traces the stretchmark braille of her belly,
searching for answers.

She cannot talk about her breasts
that still leak betrayal everyday
like clockwork.

AFTERBIRTH

Some women cradle babies
like they were born knowing how.

You hold yours like a small bomb,
the trigger,
the deep wanting in her eyes
searching for you even in the dark.

You pray, cry,
hold your breath till dizzy.
You beat your rib cage until you bruise,
but the bird in your chest
will not stop fluttering its wings.

The metal edge of her wail
curls into cage
and there you are at the center of it,
every time the baby cries.

BIRTHDAY

Mother ate the placenta
for six days after we were born
to chase the darkness
from her bones,
to quiet her wailing heart.

They say we suckled with a raging hunger
for a thing with no name,
breast milk curdled with grief.
We wept like mourning women
who already knew she would not stay.

Some days
it feels like only a small redemption
that she did not drags us with her
into the river's greedy mouth.

Most days
we are a cruel reincarnation,
a ruthless haunting
that even a father's love
cannot banish

OLEANDER

The oleander was the first to bloom
after *Little Boy* touched the heart of Hiroshima.
They said nothing would grow
for seventy years
in that city with an atom bomb on its breath.
But there are weeds that spring up
from places once thought dead,
roots that reach down
to hold still what trembles.

In the aftermath of labor,
there's a kind of quiet that passes
like the sudden hush over a shell-shocked city.
Long after the first guttural cry
from a body split open,
after the scramble for limbs and reason.

The answer to a question
no one dared to ask: a child
wrought from dust and ash,
a pink petal mouthed girl
unfurling in her mother's arms
like the poison red defiance
of a single flower
blooming on barren land.

LESSONS IN SUMMER II

This first memory is not my own,
it is my sister's retold
often enough that I enter it
and I am her
thrashing beneath the water in my uncle's pool,
every cell in my body willing itself
to float.

Inside the wide orbs of her eyes,
I learn that dying is such a silent thing
and water too has hands
that can reach around your neck and turn
your own body against you.

In the next memory
my father stands over her,
a desperate knocking on her chest,
his fingers in her mouth begging her
to open, to breathe.

And then I am a wild scream
in a public pool,
the instructor's hands squeeze
then let go,
my own five-year-old body
a flail in the deep end.
I crawl out gasping each time,
just long enough
to catch a breath
before the instructor pushes
me back again.

I learn to swim
in a violent summer that breaks
my body in,
emerge a girl who knows
how a mouth is silenced by water,

how her body can be both
anchor and life jacket.

When I am pushed under again
I teach myself a new trick
repeat it aggressively
again and again
my father's hand become my own
against my chest
and I beat and beat
until the water lets me go.

No

Your baby's first word is *no*.

Her aunties are stunned by her command
of the word,
they laugh at the boldness of how
she cradles it in her chubby cheeks
before it falls from her toothless mouth.

Only you know the months of meditation
on your hands and knees,
hours spent worshiping at the altar
of your daughter's clueless face,
begging her into an understanding.

Only you know the soft work
of pulling the word gently
from her throat, whole and intact.

A tiny weapon, the first of many
to keep the child alive.

FEAST

Inside your mother's kitchen
is a boiling pot,
inside the pot
all the things she will forgot
to teach you about becoming.

Forgive her,
she is a starving woman too
and you're old enough
to feed yourself now.

THINGS
WE LEARNED
BY BLOOD

THE VILLAGE

They call me the daughter of a dark continent,
as if we were not born
with electricity in our veins,
as if our bodies were not a conduit for light.

Even with a severed mother tongue,
we cast anchors down our throats
to find a waterlogged language, hidden
in the belly of a sinking ship,
when we first knew that even skin had a voice
that could send an SOS to God.

We have weathered greater storms,
have ridden the backs of waves
that threatened to split us in two.

These are the women that birthed me,
who taught me to spit the milk teeth
from my mouth,
let a whole continent bloom on my tongue,
and speak the stories that began
in my mother's womb.
Stories I scraped clean from her insides,
passed down through fluid vibrations,
a rhythm I could never shake.

I am stitched together
by the hands of the village that raised me,
kept whole by their best intentions.
These women and their impossible dreams
stripped bare of metaphor,
an unlikely survival story,
the daughter of a relentless love.

THINGS WE LEARNED BY BLOOD

In the photograph
his arm is draped over her shoulder.

He wears the arrogance of his youth,
a smile that shows
he has everything, even the girl
they said he could not have,

and your mother is glowing
like she knows it too.

You want to dive into her open mouth
and hear her voice
before the children,
before the baggage and the journey
across the world
that nearly broke their backs.

No one could have told her then
there was anything bigger
than this love,
or that she would spend the rest
of her life chasing this moment.

The woman in the photograph
would have laughed at the idea
she would one day have a daughter
for each finger on her hand,

that each would point an accusation,
and one would rot clean off the bone,

choose a severing so complete
the sound of her heart breaking
would echo across generations.

THE LIGHTHOUSE

We can almost set the clock by his pacing
from balcony to bedroom,
from morning to night,
when he retreats into a room
with a lock and a key he keeps in his pocket.

We have never been on the inside.
No one can describe what broken books
line the dusty shelves,
what kind of darkness grips his mind,
what corner houses his terrors,
what he runs from
trying to find stillness each night,
only to return every day.
Back and forth
from balcony to bedroom,
morning to night.

On the good days,
he is a storyteller,
he is a laughter that reaches the eyes,
he is his mother's son.
His scars are only milestones
on the road that leads back
to the womb of my grandmother's house.

Her love is umbilical,
his only anchor.
When his serpent tongue
is bloated with venom,
when his mind is more hurricane than home,
my grandmother's mouth is a lighthouse.

The neighbors who have grown accustomed
do not even watch when they come for him,
pull him rigid and fearful into the hospital van.

They know he always returns,
a shipwrecked traveler
searching for familiar light.

QUAKE

Sometimes the earth just opens
like a laughing mouth.

Had you not stayed with him
into the morning
into an afternoon
when the sun was a jealous lover,

had you not let him
shake the ghost from your bones
held his hand down a quiet street
shared a kiss
under a flickering streetlight,

had you not danced
been nothing like your mother
in a red dress
nowhere near your knees,

had you not gathered your
shoes in hand
and slipped quietly into the streets
the night before a whole city
folded like a deck of cards

they would not have found you
when the excavators arrived
flipping wall after wall like a gamble
the tremor of a smile
frozen to your lips
two bodies still fused
like a promise.

The Dream

Last night
I had a dream inside a dream.

You were there
too, my hand in yours.
You peeled my fingers open,
my palm the pink center of a rose
reaching for the sun.

Your lips, a soft petal push
against my wrist
everything springing to life
and blooming
in the brown earth of my face.

You said my name
but it was not mine.
You said my name and it was every other name.

I woke up and you were gone.
The second waking, the cruelest trick of all.

THE GARDEN
After Megan Falley

When I wasn't writing
I was tending a garden
with my teeth,
pulling up the weeds.

They come up faster
than I can chew
with roots that reach down to choke
what dares to bloom.

I swallow one called
Mother's Milk,
named for daughter's who inherit
grief with their first breath.

I name the plant with poison
after all the women I have been
and pick clean the thorns
that still spring up
from trying to love a boy
with a hole in his chest.

I turn everything over on its head
and pray a poem up from what is left.

Forgive me the mess I made.
I was trying to dig my way back to you.

Vanishing

I know how a good-natured girl
turns witch,
how the knotted sight of two bodies
taking hold
makes her monstrous.

Long after I should have forgotten
our favorite song,
it is still an elegy that troubles
the dazzling ghost of what we buried,
all that was well
and living here, gone.

I haunt the house
where we planted roses on the roof,
turn our love letters into daggers
to disappear the children we did not have.
The ribbons in their hair
crumble to dust in my hands.

On our bed, her hands draw you
back in, lips parted into a red moan
that peels the floor boards open
and I join the legion
of broken-hearted women
who slip into the earth
where your feet touch the ground.

BLOOD REMEMBERS

In the end
it was not the way his words cut
into you like shards of glass
that made you leave.

It was the memory of the revolving door
of your mother's heart,
the way your father always came back
with a suitcase filled with guilt

to find her open and waiting
with a fresh face
as though she had not yet been bruised
like rotten fruit.

NEW CHAPTER

Years from now we will pass
on a busy street,
when you are somebody's husband.

We'll graze arms like strangers
and spark a memory that will bend
our bodies back in time,
into a night when we made love
like the world was ending. It was.

We will never be those people again,
fused like a promise that would not hold,
pressed together like praying palms
to a God who had already chosen.

Later that night,
I'll search through the book
you once gave me, slide my fingers
down page after page
on the other side of town,
as your wife's knees fall open
like a new chapter.

GHOST

You loved a ghost so hard
it swallowed your heart, bloodied
your hands to polish its face
till it shone back a mirror reflection.

You kissed that shadow into being.
Taught it to feel, laugh,
speak human-like.

No one ever taught you
the alchemy of your love, its magic
animates the bones
of even the most fossilized.

The Woman Is Not Your Mother

Not mammy or wet nurse,

not a place to cut your teeth,
to milk the marrow from bone,

to suckle until sagging.
The woman is not your training wheel,

is not the leather and lust
of your first car,

is not your youthful mistake,
some "boys will be boys" story,

something hot you swallow
to put hair on your chest.

The woman is not your rite of passage,
not a river you cross to prove yourself,

carrying all your baggage on your head.
The woman is not a dumping ground.

She is not wilted and broken,
the junkyard scrap you drag home to fix.

The woman is not your project,
not your problem,

not an exercise in patience.

The woman is not a game of chance,
a choice at the cross roads of your life.

She is not a gamble.
The woman is not your lucky number,

the woman is not a reward,
she is not a trophy.

The woman is not your God,
she is not your savior or salvation,

a name you call upon like a prayer,
your last chance at forgiveness.

The woman is not your penance
for the sins of your father.

The woman is not a sin.
She is not yours, is not waiting

for permission or validation.
She is not ducking beneath her hurt.

She is not afraid to heal
or be healed.

The woman is not afraid
of her lonely, or alone.

The woman is busy in the work
of becoming whole and unto herself.

She is in conversation
with God, translating the blueprint

of creation. The woman is making
magic; she is working.

And if she finds you working too,
she might just let you love her.

HOMEGOING

HOMEGOING

All water has a perfect memory and is forever trying to get back to where it was.
—Toni Morrison

And the water still remembers the taste
of metal and blood,
of black bodies glistening like oil,
of babies thrown overboard
into its frothing mouth.

And if the ocean between two bodies of land
is a sound,
aren't we then an eight-hundred-year-old wail
between our splayed bodies,
the Atlantic slicing a jagged wound through us?

Aren't we then the moan of a cracked continent,
of a language lost in a gurgle beneath the ships,
a history bludgeoned to pulp
by the same hands that build a wall
to push us back into the remains?

Isn't our desperate voyage
along the same route our ancestors bled
then a cry that troubles the ocean floor,
reanimates the bones fossilized by rage,
a cry so wounded
that our foremother parts the sea
to call us back into her womb?

TRIGGER WARNING

Across the world
black bodies genuflect on sidewalks
to a God that is all brimstone
and fire,
their chorus
a hallelujah of bullets,
a red sea deep enough
for black mothers to swim in.

They said he looked like a serial offender,
there was too much Africa in his skin.
Something about the way he walked
screamed rape and pillage.
The way he pulled that wallet quick
out of his pocket,
it might as well have been a bullet.

     Amadou Diallo
     Trigger Warning

How dare he roar with laughter so big,
joy he didn't even have to pay for,
teeth a row of defiant white.
Now his bride is wailing in her wedding dress,
grief is a bitter liquor
fifty shots
no chaser.

     Sean Bell
     Trigger Warning

To a black woman,
a safe space might as well be a metaphor,
when she carries her body like an apology
turned inward from a gaze that is not her lover's.
She is accustomed to the rise of the hairs
on the back of her neck in response

to the scent of danger in the wind.
Even in her wounded hour,
death could still be waiting
on the other side of that door.

    Knock knock
    who's there?

    Renisha McBride
    Trigger Warning

They said he walked
they said he ran,
that it was frightening
the way he did exactly
as he was told.
They said he reached,
said he didn't reach.
Said she moved,
said she didn't move.
Said she talked back,
said she wouldn't say a word.
Said even a black boy child
wasn't child enough to play
in the broad light of an afternoon
or sit in a car seat
with gums still too soft
to speak the words for surrender:

    please
    officer
    don't
    shoot

They said cellphones kill too.
Skittles become daggers,
wallets become hand grenades and

did you know
black women fly?
Are prone to levitating
in prisons cells,
will slip their necks
into nooses they tie

with just their teeth.
All that black girl magic
defies physics,
defies gravity,
defies police officers who play God.

It turns to rage in the bones
and black bones liquefy,
slip out of handcuffs
pop locking.
They dare dance
through the trigger's warning,
dare to move in bodies that
charm a bullet out of its chamber
to sit between their eyes.

Black joy looks too much like God,
too much like worship,
too much like praise.
So give them a chorus,
a hallelujah of bullets.

Flood the streets with a red sea
deep enough
for their mothers to drown in.

This Is How You Heal The Wound

I.

Cleanse
with salt water
it is the only way
to release the poison

II.

You will need to apply
a healing balm
more
more love
be generous in your application

III.

Let the wound breathe
do not cover it until it
festers and rots
speak it
then let it go

IV.

Uncover.
Do not ever pick the scab.

OPEN

I opened my mouth
and found an amen
pulled from the throats of women
searching for the heart of God

I opened that amen
and found my grandmother's
praying hands
calloused from years of raising children
that were not her own

I opened her hands
and found a mustard seed
still small and intact
ready to spring from within itself

I opened the seed
and found her heart
still warm and beating
love rushing from chamber to chamber

I opened her heart
and found a story
about forgiveness
about starting over
about letting go
about love

I opened her story
and found my mouth
ready and waiting to tell it

I opened my mouth
and found an amen

again and again and again

GOLD

They say
Itoro has a goldmine between her legs,

the men who go digging do not come out
until she is done with them.

Once we saw a governor
at her doorstep with only his briefs on,
his childish cries loud and unashamed.

They say her people know how to love well,
that her mother showed her how
to swallow a man whole,
how to hold his heart in her hand
and squeeze
until he begs to be reborn inside her.

Sometimes we catch a glimpse of her
naked on her balcony,
her body spilling over with softness.
Incandescent in the moonlight,
oblivious to our hungry eyes.

On those nights our husbands ask
what came over us,
why we howl like wild women
who learned to spin gold
with just our hips.

ELEGY

It frightens you,
the way she moves
like she alone created rhythm.

She braids her hair
with strands of lightening,
smiles like she knows the secrets of the moon,
calls the sun by its real name,
a shared fire between them.

When she works, honey bees
pause to watch her.
Thunder claps when she laughs,
the wind nudges the branches
to bow for her.

And when she is done loving
she digs her teeth into the sutures,
wants the scars with the healing,
feels the pebbles beneath her fingers,
counts each lover like a prayer bead,
chants a love poem
like a prayer for the dead.

CREATION STORY

Before light was first spoken
we existed,
in the moment before Genesis,
before the taste of forbidden fruit,
as a speck of dust.

We know this darkness well.
Move through it with the speed
of love or light,
your ribs a creation blueprint beneath
my fingers, your mouth a holy place,
a thousand amens.

You unearth me, travel over me
like a pilgrimage, each heartbeat a prophecy.
We are a creation story,
a testament to weathering storms two by two,
the audacity to walk on water
and take down giants.

I only need look for the miracles
in your smile
to remember that there is salvation in a kiss,
small mercies in a pulse.

They will call this blasphemy,
say we spit in the face of holiness,
the way we worship.
But there is no greater proof
of God than this,
no closer to divine than us:
the Lazarus rise of a stack of bones,
red seas parting in our veins.

We are light at the frequency
of everything, the promise of eternity
whispered into the night.

BONES

Centuries from now
when the archaeologists
shake the dust from your bones,
let them wonder about this thing
called courage.
Let them still find traces
of brave and beautiful.

When they rearrange each part,
hold you piece by piece
against the light,
give them a scar to marvel at.

Let their history books say:

Here lies a woman who knew
that fear is just a growling animal
with no teeth.

LAUGHTER ECHOES LIKE FORGIVENESS

Only the ocean holds a grudge here,
heavy with the rumor
of broken bodies
of blood and bone
beneath brick and mortar.

The children laugh easy here,
cheeks glistening like ripe fruit
beneath a smiling sun,

bodies bounce the same rhythm
the familiar music they make
with their hands and feet.

Their joy is loud and unapologetic,
oblivious to the noise
of the ocean crashing into the shoreline
again and again
with the rage of an unrequited love.

THIS IS HOW WE DISAPPEAR

This is how we disappear:
we fall backwards into our mother's mouths,
become them,
become the only stories we have ever been told.
Stories about women who stay,
women who offer up their bodies
into the belly of the beast
to protect their children.

This is how we go missing:
we tumble into a fist,
bones beaten to pulp.
Crumble beneath the weight
of a man with a hole in his chest
and the vacuum takes us
to a place where we are never enough,
yet we are too much.
Our mouths too big,
bodies too soft,
too whole.

So the wolves come,
dragging the screeching bodies
of little girls from their childhoods,
folding our heart into their mouths.
They find us at work, at school,
knees bent at the altar or on the dance floor.
Whether we are a shy whisper or a loud joy,
whether we are hips loose and free
or too small to carry the weight of it.

They come with a stranger's whisper
or with names we know well.
We call them uncle,
call them brother,
call them friend.
Call them on nights when the world feels too big,

when we ask for a shoulder and get a fist instead,
claws that peel our bodies open.

We try to forget what we cannot forgive,
we throw away our names.
We shape shift,
code switch,
tell no one,
hold the secret in our mouths until it rots.
We cancer in silence,
learn a whole new language for survival,
teach it to our daughter's too.

But today we take our voices back,
take our bodies back.
We gather the broken,
gather the split and scattered,
gather what remains,
whatever still has a pulse.
Even what is only a shadow of itself
is still worth of loving.

Everything we paid for in our blood,
let it come. From all the places
we were left for dead, we return
with nothing but the skin on our backs.

We do not glance back,
we do not turn to salt this time.
We are ocean.
We reclaim what belongs to us
and we swallow whatever refuses to be moved.

Ask about us,
these women who reinvented joy,
who snapped back our broken bones
to the rhythm of a survival song.
A song about the audacity of living
and loving anyway.

We become a new kind of creature,
something fearless and fierce,
something bold enough to call down
even lightening
and dare it to touch us.

THE CROSSING

My great-grandmother sits
under the shade of a cocoa tree,
sweat glistening on the bridge of her nose.

The seeds of an age-old language fall
from her lips,
a dense forest springs up at her feet.

My tongue is a machete
clearing a path to find her waiting
barefoot at a bridge she has built
just for me to travel the river of my becoming.

I genuflect ẹ ṣe mama
and we cross over.

NOTES

"Missing"

The first section is a found piece from quotes in the *Associated Press* article, "A year after kidnap of schoolgirls in Nigeria, hope dwindles" (April 15, 2015).

The third and fourth section of the poem are found pieces from the *New Yorker* article, "The Desperate Journey of a Trafficked Girl," by Ben Taub (April 10, 2017).

"Hide and Seek"

The quote "They give you food, but in the night they come back." is a quote from "Ama," an internally displaced woman living in the Bama Hospital Camp, interviewed for the Amnesty International Report, "They Took Our Husbands and Forced Us to Be Their Girlfriends— Women In North-East Nigeria Starved and Raped by Those Claiming to Rescue Them" (September 2018).

ACKNOWLEDGMENTS

For the women. For the girls. For those we name and those we cannot. For the storm that brews in the butterfly effect of your migration patterns across the globe.

For my family, by blood or bond, my sisters, my best friends, Motik Ng. With you I am always whole.

For the village, the first storytellers, my grandmothers, my aunties, my mother, with one hand reaching for God, the other one right here, doing the work. You showed me disappearance as magic making, as survival, as reinvention, too. Thank you.

For my husband, Oluwaseun. Your love is a lighthouse. Thank you for always pointing me toward home.

For the wild wonder of motherhood and my first true poem, Teniolu, The Best Boy In The World, who was birthed alongside this book. Thank you for choosing me.

For my Rouge Poetry and Breath in Poetry Collective family who gave my poems a home in Edmonton. For Ahmed "Knowmadic" Ali, who kept the dream alive so I could go in search of a thing I didn't even have the language for yet. Thank you.

For my yard people, who gave my poems a home in Lagos, and the impromptu writing group where some of these poems first emerged: Efe Paul Azino, Wana Udobang, Chika Jones, Dami Ajayi, Obii Ifejika, Lebo Mashile (our honorary Nigerian). I know no better cabal than one that pushes you deeper into your truth and your craft. Thank you.

Thank you Rachel McKibben's for the revelation that was the Red Pen Heaven workshop. It showed me what was possible. Thank you Xandria Phillips for the first edit that broke the book open.

Thank you Brad Morden and the Write Bloody North family. Thank you Alessandra Naccarato, the most amazing editor, for being the blade and the balm. For pushing me to carve the monster of this manuscript until its true face emerged. Thank you for seeing me (and it) well.

Thank you to the Canada Council for the Arts for supporting the creation of this collection through the Professional Development for Artists Grant.

Early versions of these poems have appeared on *Brittle Paper*, DamiAjayi.com, and in the *Soaring Africa Anthology* (OSIWA) and *Abscess* (Geko Publishing).

About the Author

TITILOPE SONUGA is a writer and performer who calls Lagos, Nigeria, and Edmonton, Canada, home. The recipient of the Canadian Authors' Association Emerging Writer Award, and a 2015 Open Society (OSIWA) Foundation Resident Poet on Goree Island, off the coast of Senegal, she is a leading voice in local and international performance poetry communities who has travelled extensively as a poet and facilitated poetry workshops across the world. Her poetry has been translated into Italian, German and Slovak.

titilope.ca

Write Bloody North publishes groundbreaking voices and legends of spoken word to create innovative, fresh poetry books.

We believe that poetry can change the world for the better. We are an independent press dedicated to quality literature and book design. We are grassroots, DIY, bootstrap believers. Pull up a good book and join the family. Support independent authors, artists, and presses.

Want to know more about Write Bloody North books, authors, and events? Join our mailing list at

www.writebloodynorth.ca

CPSIA information can be obtained
at www.ICGtesting.com
Printed in the USA
BVHW082137270819
556946BV00001B/63/P

9 780992 024536